D0927492

With Akhmatova at the Black Gates

With Akhmatova

FOREWORD BY

HAYDEN CARRUTH

University of Illinois Press

Urbana / Chicago / London

at the Black Gates

VARIATIONS

Stephen Berg

Also by Stephen Berg

811.54
Berg

POETRY

Poems (1954)
Bearing Weapons (1963)
The Queen's Triangle (1970)
The Daughters (1970)
Nothing in the Word: Versions of Aztec Poetry (1972)
Grief: Poems and Versions of Poems (1975)
Flutes in the Sacred City: Versions of Simonides (1977)

TRANSLATIONS

Sunstone by Octavio Paz (1958)
Clouded Sky by Miklos Radnoti
    (with Steven Polgar and S. J. Marks, 1972)
Oedipus the King by Sophocles
    (with Diskin Clay, 1978)

© 1981 by Stephen Berg
Manufactured in the United States of America
Some of these poems appeared first, at a different stage,
in *Grief: Poems and Versions of Poems* (New York:
Viking Compass, 1975), and in *The Nation, The New York
Review of Books, The Iowa Review, The New Republic.*
Library of Congress Cataloging in Publication Data
Berg, Stephen.
  With Akhmatova at the black gates.
  I. Title.
PS3552.E7W5   811'.54   80-14469
ISBN 0-252-00833-2 (cloth)
ISBN 0-252-00834-0 (paper)

To Millie, Clair, Margot, and my mother

Contents

Foreword by Hayden Carruth / *ix*

1/

Last Meeting / *3*

1909 / *4*

1911 / *5*

In the Woods / *6*

To C. M. Lozinsky, 1912 / *7*

Spring, 1912 / *8*

1914 / *9*

Roses / *10*

Shells, Stars / *11*

July / *12*

1915 / *14*

In the Park / *15*

Summer / *16*

1916 / *17*

January / *18*

Two Fragments / *19*

Two Little Songs / *20*

1922 / *21*

Nothingness / *22*

2/

Memory / 27

3/

New Year's / 37

Willow, 1940 / 38

Thread / 39

Back / 41

Tashkent Blossoms, 1944 / 42

Bezhetsk / 43

1945 / 44

October, 1959 / 45

This Cold / 47

You / 49

Fragment, 1959 / 51

After Sophocles' Death / 53

In the Evening / 54

In Two / 56

Alone / 57

My Door / 59

Endings / 61

Afterword by Stephen Berg / 65

Acknowledgments / 67

Foreword

Few people any longer doubt that the great epics and sagas of antiquity were made collaboratively. The poems were transmitted by tellers, and in the repeated tellings were revised and strengthened, both formally and substantially. When alphabets were invented, followed by the spread of what we are pleased to call "literacy," the poems were written down, but usually in variant texts that show us aspects of their development. In some cases we even see the longer process—for instance, how the powerful story of Gilgamesh in Babylonia emerged from the earlier, more childlike, and more freely inventive stories of Sumer, or how, at the other end of the line, certain folk tales of Amerindians now living in northern Guatemala are remnants and reductions of the great *Popol Vuh*. But we need not go so far from our own self-conscious tradition to see examples. Pope rewrote poems by Chaucer and Donne. Shakespeare rewrote Boccaccio and in turn was rewritten by Lamb. Fitzgerald is as clearly present as Omar in the *Rubaiyat*. Duncan has given us "versions" of Shelley and Keats. And so forth. The use of cultural references in art is not, as some anti-intellectuals think, to show off the artist's learning; nor is it, as some intellectuals think, primarily to reinforce meanings. It is to strengthen the companionship of artists living and dead so that their action may be more cogent throughout the polity. With exactly this in mind, Pound called his rewriting of Propertius an "homage."

All discussion of the legitimate or illegitimate uses of literature, especially when impelled, as it so often is, by petty righteousness, is stupid and boring. Any use is legitimate if the end is good. And today one wants to add that *almost* any use is better than none.

I have been privileged to read some of these poems by Stephen Berg, which derive from English translations of poems in Russian by Anna Akhmatova, in various drafts and to read the entire manuscript in its completion. Let me say what I think has happened. At the beginning were three distinct people: Akhmatova, the translator (sometimes more than one), and Berg himself. Beyond what I can extrapolate from their published works, and in Berg's case from a few private letters, I know nothing about any of the three. But I have been able to see in their progressive drafts how the poems have moved, not toward Akhmatova, not toward Berg, certainly not toward the translators, but instead toward a fourth separable personality, mythic and amenable. Akhmatova and Berg discovered each other, so to speak, in the English translations, and thereafter carried on a dialogue across cultures, times, and the frontier of death. It has been an acute, loving, utterly candid dialogue, from which came these poems different from any that either Akhmatova or Berg would or could have written on their own. Naturally a special affinity must have existed between these two, something more than the ordinary accession of reader to writer; but this does not mean that the rest of us cannot participate in this affinity now that its products are here on the page. These poems are a fusion of two lives, two minds, two sensibilities, and if they have been engendered in the imagination of only one, Berg's, nevertheless they derive equally from both.

Berg has done what he felt driven to do: add, subtract, rearrange, substitute his own for Akhmatova's and the translators' diction, pace, and line structure. Some poems are near the originals, some very far away. But in all cases they are poems, not translations, adaptations, free versions, or any other such transferences; and Akhmatova is in them as much as Berg. They are an homage, praise of the dead for the glorification of the living, yet to my mind a clearer homage than Pound's to Propertius because Berg has chosen his collaborator from a nearer culture and a more recent time. Manifestly Akhmatova's crisis of existence bears and evokes resemblances to our own, sharpened in Berg's case by the affinity of temperaments. Beyond this the collaborators are woman and man, a fact which is important in ways and degrees too large for this short introduction to distinguish, much less explore, though I am confident many readers will appreciate it. Above all the poems are a work of authorial collectivity. In some measure this collectivity restores to both authors the anonymity, the unfathomableness, of which real poets must always partake. I do not mean to suggest more than I say. We have lived through the eighteenth century, Locke to Voltaire to Kant to Coleridge, and we cannot rescind our Romantic and post-Romantic—or better, ultra-Romantic—reliance on individual genius; nor do I think we should. But the "equation" has been unbalanced on the side of ego for too long, which is in part responsible, I believe, for the schism between art and polity in modern civilization. This is changing. Art is once more, under the stress of current difficulties in the distribution of works to an appropriate audience, becoming socialized, not in the sense of "social realism" or any other artistic creed, but in the willingness of younger artists to accept partial anonymity and let their works express the communal, rather than the individual, personality. *With Akhmatova at the Black Gates* is one evidence, but we have more, including the tendency I have seen among my students to rewrite each other's poems, producing in effect collaborative versions. I deplore the ignorance which makes them rely on too flimsy sources, but I applaud their modesty before the muse.

Finally, an introduction is not a review. The poems are here, and readers and critics must judge them as they will. For my part I find some of them, though ultimately consoling, more than momentarily shattering in their power of human feeling and insight. This shattering is the bedrock literary achievement of western civilization in mid-century, call it what you will: existential, humanist, the resurging spirit; but above all it means the concentration of imaginative energy on the plight of ordinary human animals caught in the fateful destructiveness of their own technological and moral evolution. For this I can personally commend them to all readers, and for their betokening an important further principle especially to all critics.

Hayden Carruth

A past should be familiar enough for us

to be able to relive it automatically, yet strange

enough to astonish us each time we turn back to it:

then it is ready for our imagination.

— CESARE PAVESE

Last Meeting

I was helpless, my breasts were freezing.
I walked one foot on tiptoe,
I put my left glove on
my right hand, like an idiot.

There seemed to be so many steps then
but I knew there were only three.
Autumn whispered through the maples
"Die, like me:

that sick, truculent liar, Fate,
has stripped me, for the hell of it."
"I've been flayed like you," I remember answering
as I left, "and I'll die when you do."

This is our last meeting— this place, this voice.
I looked back at the shape of the dark house.
Candles guttered in the bedroom window;
behind them, eyes and a torso.

I haven't slept all night, both sides
of my pillow are damp and hot,
the second candle flame sputters
in its pool of wax, now
idiotic lewd shrieks of a crow
get closer, closer, the noise
grates on me, fills me, fills my room,
then nothing.
Everything's like that. Now
it's too late even to think about sleeping—
the white shade pulled down over the white window
is too white. Morning!
You: the same voice, the same look in your eyes
I saw when we first met, the same yellow hair.
Everything is as it was years ago—
we touched, time wasn't there.
The world passing outside my window is as clear
as the palm of my own hand; the blank,
whitewashed walls on all four sides are infinite,
are everything, are nothing. I can't think.
When I stare at them I go straight through.
The sweet, thick stink of lilies, cut minutes ago.
Nothing except our words.

A riding whip, a glove wait on the table,
God knows why. Who left them there?
One window's open a little.
I hear the lindens rustle.

They seem to call me.
Why did you leave? I
can't understand it. Why?
The desk lamp's cozy circle —

it focuses the pain, it lets me see again
two people shielded from the world
by love's illusion: if it lasts we can't die.
Think of us. Who were we?

Tomorrow morning's light will soothe me
like a warm hand. I know it.
I know this life is good.
Heart, don't worry —

last night I could barely hear
that hesitant, aching plea you've begun to make.
I was reading in an old book
that souls are immortal.

In the Woods

White points like stars or pinholes bore through the
     night— eyes.
The owl's and mine.
The end of the story, how
my lover died— it's not happy.

I'm stretched out on the short, moist grass
at the edge of a nearby field, singing to myself.
Words can't do anything. Neutral, intent,
the bird stares at me through its pale mask of wisdom,

seeming to listen carefully; needles and scaly
bark scratch my thighs, the sky's a gray, desolate rag.
They took him,
my so-called brothers dragged him away,

not from the trenches, not in the panic of war.
I remember seeing his footprints stop suddenly, go
     nowhere.
On this same little path through the woods,
near my house, here. The pain's incurable,

I'm burying my face in you—
this gift between endless darknesses, this life
is the taste of cold grass prickling my face
on the path that is almost invisible now.

To C. M. Lozinsky, 1912

It will never end, this heavy amber day
that drags like a chain riveted to the bands
clamped on a convict's ankles—
life is impossible, its sadness always comes back.
Expect it, don't look for anything else.

Deer cry out— their sleek, tender eyes
dazed by the Northern Lights— it sounds like a silver fork
hitting a knife
when a drawer is opened or a table set.
There are times noises like that say it all.

Once I believed each inch of snow was beautiful;
once I believed the church's blue stone font,
where the desperate and faithful kneel to drop their
        coins, made sense;
once I believed rides gliding in a sleigh through the
        night,
jolting us against each other

into a single spirit no one could hurt or separate,
would save us. Forever. Quaint flustered harness bells,
hiss of the runners, us
huddled there, rushed between black trees, moon
haloing the edges of the shape we were, *are* —

even now as I put down my glass— this mystery.

Simply, wisely— that's how I've taught myself to live.
I take long walks at twilight, I look at the sky, I pray to
    God—
that's how I drain off my restlessness, that's
how I face evening coming on.

Burdock rasp in a gully,
fat clusters of yellowish, red-freckled berries bump my
    legs—
I trudge back to the house and write poems that say
joy, decay, beauty: they shape what we call our soul.

The cat licks my palm and gurgles
and is at peace. I run my cheek across its fur. I see
one bulb swaying on the top floor
of the sawmill that hulks by the lake,

and the silence, the humming nightly silence is like the
    silence
inside me after I have prayed, and believe. Only
storks quacking, clattering as they blanket the roof
interrupt the silence. That light slashes the darkness.

Sitting here, I feel you just outside the room.
Maybe I still want you, but I don't care.
If you knocked at my door,
I wouldn't hear you, I wouldn't even be home.

It's here again, it moves, its tin-white scythe
flashes through the pinkish fur of tall weeds,
the *wockwock wockwock* of unshod hooves is coming
    closer.
Don't tell me you don't care about sleep either,
don't say you can't forget me,
can't make love in your own bed, alone now one whole
    year.

The moon offers its mottled, steady blade.
It stops. It makes a scar on the darkness. Darkness: the
    strangler.
Hoofbeats again, dream trace, memory, twin faces—
    us?— the one answer
a bitter tone in your voice, louder, louder:
sitting up all night in a chair till the sky turns white
and wakes my chilly room, I can't breathe, I see
    everything, know everything:

two or three words,
the words,
lost, like a breath,
the elation of a truth
I heard, saw, need again
but still can't quite remember.

Roses

Can you still stand on the edge of the Neva
and watch it move,
can you still walk out under the lamps and look down
from the bridges and stare until the waters blur and
    merge with you
and you lift your arms off the green iron railings
and shake yourself back?
I see your face above and in the water,
a man, yes, but part of me says a god;
and I still feel your mouth, opening to mine,
our tongues greeting each other;
and part of me still feels
grass, leaves, and flowers will die forever
each time snow simplifies the land.
One love, one life, one face in that river.
There's a reason I'm so sad
since the first time I saw you in a dream,
saw you hover then lie next to me in bed
then disappear like mist sucked out of my room.
Whenever you come back— more often now— I'm like a
    child:
angels have wings honed fine as a razor,
the end of the world is almost here— look!—
fires the size of a fist break out everywhere on the snowy
    hills,
blood roses puncturing that white, white skin.

Shells, Stars

The road's a black gash
between the garden and the sea.
The sea is growing darker.
Everywhere shells,
outlining flower beds, sandy paths, scattered,
everywhere stars.
There's a weird glow coming from both at this hour
just past twilight— luminous blue the vein-blue of the
    sky—
shells cupping the sand or open to the sky, star-
light reaching us, at last, year after year.
The lamps are yellow and clear,
but I still see nights when the fog veiled everything—
houses, streets, the hoarse, absolute sea—
and hazy balls something like milkweed
seemed fixed in the air where the lamps were.
When I look up past the spiny, bleak tips
of the pine tops, through raw, unintended holes
in the weave of needle and branch,
and see sky
I know only one thing:
I can trust you, we'll be friends,
take walks, age together— and this:
because we love each other death's nothing—
stars foaming in seas and patches, men, beasts
striding, kneeling, growling, crawling, all
eighty-eight alive with their human names.

There's a stench of burning, dry peat smolders in the
   bogs.
Four weeks of it. Even the birds won't sing today, the
   snakes won't leave their holes.
God hates us. You can tell by how hot the sun is. Not a
   drop of rain
on the fields since Easter, not a sprinkle. A one-legged
   stranger came by,
and, ranting in the courtyard, said,

"The worst is coming. Fresh graves will pack the earth.
   Hunger, earthquakes, plagues,
the eclipse of heavenly bodies— the enemy will rip our
   land apart for his pleasure,
but the Mother of God will draw her white veil across
   our pain. I know it."
From the woods the sweet, chilly air of juniper floats in.
Soldiers' wives play with their children and moan.

Widows are sobbing all across the village. But our prayers
weren't wasted. The earth needed rain so the trampled
   fields were soaked
by a warm, scarlet rain. The sky is so close to us, so blank
   and bare
that the voice of someone at prayer is nothing but a
   whisper—
"They're stabbing Your holy body, gambling for Your
   robe!"

Everything's looted, betrayed, sold. Death's jagged wing
   flashes before us,

within us. Everything's eaten by anguish, and eaten
    again.
Lights are kept going for us, though. Why?
Each day odors of the cherry blow in from a secret farm
    near the town,
each night new constellations appear

and the miraculous grazes our ruined, filthy houses —
a thing nobody, not one of us, has ever known, a thing
    nobody recognizes.
A boy plays some instrument. A girl slips bluebells in her
    hair. Me? You?
Low fires still patiently burn in the distance.

These.

I'm sick. I hear the cranes
call over the icy fields,
their wings pale gold underneath
in the crumbling, muggy light,

their wings a dense, low cloud
the color of the brushwood
stacked years ago against my house.
Brown? Gray? I say to the cranes

the gold on their wings is the river's.
They can't hear me, of course, but I speak.
They swerve. Their wings rumble.
They shadow rock dynamiters blasted back

all along one hillside to put a road in.
That first time we touched naked I kissed you there.
Pockets and cracks of snow melt in the rocks.
Ten feet away winter-puffed sparrows

land in a birch that's as tall as I am,
stay for a minute, scoot off when I touch my hair.
I feel the river inside me, thawing, alone. Its heaviness.
In this fever your sweet, moist, pubic tangle.

In the Park

The meadow is brown, it reaches the dim sky.
The water's poisonous, scummy.
I'll never forget how it looks today,

I'll never forget how close we were
when we'd visit there and hide
all afternoon, till dark, like bad children.

When you pass through the filigreed iron gate—
    no lock—
joy shoots up through your whole body.
You're not alone, not really.

Your life has changed. Late fall.
Wind shifting, crisp, arrogant, free.
On this side of the gate you forget how it weighs.

Pines glittering with frost; pocked, muddy lumps of snow.
Hill, palace, park— are they real?
No spearheads decorating the gate, no brass crest—

benches, a few dry fountains, pony rides.
We were so close how will I ever miss you?
On one shoulder of the blind bronze statue

of a couple like us
a bird with a red, fluttering breast.
I can't stop looking at its throat.

Summer

Whatever I looked at told me you'd be mine:
a hazy, red, thin scarf of cloud,
tattering inches above the trees;
my dream of Christmas morning, still months away;

winds at Easter crisscrossing like the voices of all the
     people I know;
stiff, rubbery shoots pimpling the vine;
the park with its waterfalls; two
fat dragonflies, dozing and awake

on one post of the rusted iron fence.
Now the last leaves scuttle away;
when we hold hands and skate into the distance
over the gray slushy ice on the lake, feeling we'll reach
     the sky,

I know this:
we'll be friends, you'll be the friend I think of
as I pace all the slopes of the last hill
and feel the hot stones push up through my shoes.

Not a boat or cart
can bring you here,
wherever you step deep pools
gnaw at the rotting snow.
Nothing can help
this farm cut off on all sides
by the constant shocks of cold.
Someone I love
is dying nearby, of love.
He gets up, drags himself to the sledge,
checks it, waxes the runners,
quiets the horses,
slumps back on the couch. There,
he waits for me, falls asleep. One spur
catches in the rug
and rips it down the middle.
A finger of sallow floor shows through.
It's all treachery.
It's finished.
One of us sees the other, in his mind. Any image will do:
kneeling in a trench; cooking; walking the field where
    sky peeps through
the lacy bare-branched tops of oaks woven above the
    hillside behind this house.
Not a mirror in the house
knows your face—so warm, so gentle—oh I want to
but I can't live off the joy of seeing you smile
in even a single snapshot, in one plate or windowpane.

1
The snowdrift doesn't collapse, it's packed hard
as we walk its crest to my lone, mysterious house,
aware of how quiet we are, aware
of the tenderness in the silence between us.
I'm naked, in bed, waking, sleeping;
my thoughts float anywhere, with you.
The Book is closed. I like its silent pages.
No song ever sung was lovelier than this—
this dream I am having, looking out, and in . . .
how twigs snap back when our legs catch the bushes,
how lulling the chime of your spurs is, killingly cheerful.

2
No one lives in the house with me,
ice shrinks on the creaking roof,
but I don't count these lost, meaningless days.
I pick up the Book and read in the Apostles,
I measure David's lines of praise.
The stars look blue, frost
fuzzes the bricks, stalks, tree trunks, gates . . .
whatever exists touches something else.
I love seeing that; it's a miracle!
I find the Song of Songs—
a red leaf marks it: still shiny; the size of a baby's hand:
    maple.

Two Fragments

I wake early
from a dream of happiness that strangles me,
I look out the portholes at the waves,
green with sizzling white claws on top,
I go out on deck— there's a moon—
wrapped in a wool coat,
it drizzles as I listen to the engines mumbling,
my heart and theirs together—
I can't tell which is mine.
That way I don't need to think about anything
though I feel I'll meet you again;
I grow younger by the minute,
the salt spray, the winds slashing my face.
An image wavers before my face.

I don't see my childhood any more.
I don't see butterflies mating in air
the way I used to when I was sixteen.
Horrible how the moon spreads its chalky glow
on the sky, on the sea— town after town
poisoned, the people bent with pain:
they want death
because of the sick laws of tyrants. That's what I see.
You're gone. That's why I sing and dream.
One day I woke and the whole world was silent.
The guns had stopped.
My heart slowed, I could barely move.
Death Patrols rummaged every house except mine.

Two Little Songs

1

How many years will I live?
I asked the sparrow.
The pine tops shivered,
a narrow plank of sunlight struck the grass.
Not a sound. The raw, welcoming smell
of earth, of leaves, of whatever it is
from childhood centuries old, soaking in these woods,
and nothing else.
Now I am walking home—
a ruffle of wind cools
the tight, hot skin of my forehead.

2

I used to say nothing all morning
about what my dream told me.
For me, for the rose,
for the day's first light there's only one fate:
to be the music that is everywhere
heard *in* things, *as* things.
Snow crumbles and slides down the hills,
I'm as fragile as snow,
solid as the banks of swollen, muddy rivers—
the pungent roar of the pine thicket
is more peaceful than my thoughts at dawn.

No cool, moist breezes, not a cloud
shadowing the flat glass dome of the sky
that fall— September almost gone,
everyone shocked by its heat and color.
Thorns, roses, rocks, everything smelled heavy,
red sunsets choked the air, torturing us,
the dirty canal turned green.
We will see this until we are all dead.
The sun came back again, again, and again,
taking the capital, capturing the throne.
Sometimes nobody moved for hours.
There was a silence in which rich and poor
were one. Not a grain of dust, not a leaf lifted.
That autumn
scorched every face and brick. Whiffs of snow.
I still see one of those
moments of pure equality— I was standing next to
a horse,
I could hear its whinnying sneezes, smell its flanks, see
a soldier's boots beneath its barrel, the back of his head
          where
the cap pinched his hair; links of bright metal.
I thought: I will see you until the day I die.
I went home, bathed; washed and braided my hair.
And that was when you came to my door.
I opened it. You looked at me. Your eyes
were cool and without hope like a leaf that has lost its
          color.

Nothingness

I want to be sick, I want to meet everyone again
in my fever, I want to walk the wide streets
of the glary, seaside garden, scoured by the wind,
and forget. Nothing has happened before this.

The dead and exiled walk into my house. I want each
    child
brought to me by the hand. I miss them.
When I was a child my nurse's hand was always right
    there
above my hand. I'd reach up and clutch her finger.

I'm going to eat grapes
with the children I love, drink cold white wine,
watch the waterfall spill
bleakly over and over across my flint bed. But I still see

a house where I was taken to a cell and questioned,
led back, and I won't say what else. Now I am waking,
why am I crying, everyone loses everyone, everything.
It's done now, but my dreams— nothing

of my life in them, nothing. I do recognize ordinary
    things,
and rooms, people, vaguely; to be in a world completely
new is to lose everything. But I can see the waves and
    feel the sun
and smell the salt in the air that lurches and halts, gently.

I sit in my room. On the wall in front of me, the Cross.
    Nothing else.

It's as if I had never seen it before. Its hacked, blackish,
equal pieces of unstained, trashed wood hold Him up
    there. Body
of ivory. Flies land on my foot and stay there.

2/

I'm here; it's here,
I'm not sure which is which:
sky red as a fresh knife wound, sky
of fire, abyss, my home
reviving in me after all these years
as voices, creaking wagons, the *plock*
of a butcher's cleaver passing through bone
into the block of maple,
returning from the afterlife, eternal, strange,
blood inside and out,
blood everywhere . . .

a clock face changing as the sun
circles the sky
but in me also, without hands
or numbers.

All my life
I've been terrified this would happen:
autumn:
the world, my soul—
as if everything I fought against
inside me all my life
isn't part of me now,
is the stone, leaves, flowers
of these blind walls and this small garden,
as distant as your lips are from my lips. . . .

Invisible; visible.
I don't know what the difference is.
I don't mean God, religion.
I've spent my whole life writing

clear, simple sentences, things that I felt.
Love. Loss. Bitterness. Exaltation.
But mostly tenderness—
that astonishing mood we grown-ups call "the essence of
    things,"
Babel says, describing how he felt as a child walking
    down his hometown streets—
no matter how hard life became, how dead
the heart felt, whipped
by its quest for love.

Impossible; possible . . .
they called my name
then took me to a wooden room.
I laughed inappropriately; a second Akhmatova went:
one peeked through neighbors' windows, picked flowers,
rambled the beach, read all day on a rock,
waves nibbling at her feet;
and one, in a chair bolted to the floor,
said anything. Anything. Or did she? Innocent. Sincere.
Like a child pacifying its mother.

Whoever I was, I'm here now— *here*— God!
beyond my past, not there, still there
unless these homeless voices I am are
that betrayed, nameless nothingness in rags freezing
for nineteen months beside you, *you,*
prisoner, witness, women of silence— here,
Leningrad. And someone said "I can." These numb
    words go
like beggars, knocking at gates, and get no answer.

———

Death. Nothing. Nothing after death.
Right now when I look back over my shoulder
into the room where I sleep and write

I see my old house following me, its
one vacant, malicious, hollow eye
of light all night long gnawing through the wall,
    the darkness.
Fifteen years. Forever. Dense as granite.
Akhmatova: Granite: Time:
the verge of revelation— that the past
can't be held or measured, that it changes,
that it's as strange to me as it would be
to my neighbor if he could see it, hear it, taste it.

Late one night
I couldn't sleep. I dressed and went outside and
    stretched out in the cold grass
behind my house
where the dry, scrambled, black stalks clicked,
tangling against the sky, and the barn hulks stood out,
    infinitely serene,
the entire world far in the distance —
stars, clouds.
What were those cores of light, that surf of yearning
    formlessness
doing there, what were they trying to say?
I thought I could hear them speaking to me

it was the voice of millions,
a voice above our meeting,
a voice muttering nothing I understood
to the one I left,
as if my own voice stunned me when it came
from God knows where, one uninterrupted, unidentified
    scream. . . .

———

There's a house, I'm not sure where.
In it fine, brown dust has thickened on everything,

in it the woman I was still clings to the man
who could have killed me, we were so close,
I was so young and lost in my love for him.
That flat, grayish-brown light of just-before-winter
still dulls things there, a sign of nonexistence.
And there are times, writing this, trying to know
what to say, when whole pages
from unsent letters fill my head
as if the only life I really have is in the truth of passion
I can never let you know . . .

wind enters the chimney and it sounds like me
or like the person in those letters
or like all the changes made in these lines
or like the men and women who still march back
to that house where . . .

what good are details?

———

An inkstain
no one bothered to wipe off
my bleached oak dining-room table,
a kiss
so hard I still feel bone against bone at times, again,
        again until I believe
love *is* eternal, love is the one law,
the same spider I saw in that house
motionless on its web right there
across from me as I say this and reach to touch . . .

the clock, a tear, these moments of you. . . .

I'm awake now:
shame, anger, inescapable revenge.
The road that led to me here

unrecognizable. Nobody knows us.
The city burns, old fires sputter out, finally,
1942. With a lamp and a bunch of keys
glittering before me, I sit at my desk, I see
the one witness I trust: my thin, crippled maple
looking in at this woman speaking,
knowing we won't meet again, offering
its dried-out, scrawny arms to me.
Tobruk rumbles through the floor
into my legs and spine and hands,
one unexpected, pure, white star looks— yes, looks—
    and sees me,
sitting alone,
not only me but everyone
who suffers with its distant, steady, pitiless way
of being here.

City I love, we'll never be apart—
when I leave, my shadow will cling to your walls,
my breasts and face tremble in your canals,
my footsteps sound in the museums,
I'll cut a path by pacing some green field
as I walk and walk, free, kneeling over the silence
of the graves my brothers lie in,
seeing their faces, tasting their tears.

The unknowable sleep of things embraces the world.
Everyone looks through a strange window.
Some live in Tashkent, some in Philadelphia
in this age of sickening, bitter air,
the air of exiles and poisons. I left—
bridges, tunnels, the Kama lidded with ice—
I took the road so many from this country died on:
my son, you, you, and you, a live, huge knotted thread
being dragged through the grim, crystal silence of Siberia
by filthy gods.

The sleep of things. What is it? Sunset or dawn,
the maple still looks in. Nobody's there, or here. Keys on
    the desk.
The woods are quiet. A handful of camp dust. This
woman still being questioned by men in uniform; this
blued revolver lifted so many times to her head—
one's own voice heard always as a miracle, each step
and detail of the world, each instant of consciousness
    impossible. . . .

I speak to the city from the other side,
not Hell or Heaven, but not from where you are,
one woman, one man, and millions,
I, who discovered how to forget even love,
who could sit looking at the ocean for weeks— there
    were no days— waiting
for the one who could split open even wider my terrified
    heart.

————

Photograph: families looking of all things shy
cupping their genitals with both hands
so we will never see— doesn't that mean they
still knew their own names?
grouped on the edge of the bottom half of the shot
that could be of the deep gray ocean
a pit that does not end with the shot
but flows out past its edges in the mind
as they try not to be there by looking as if nothing
    special
is going on
huddling in front of the amateur Sunday photographer's
    candid
visor-shaded blank eye

Photograph: whole bodies of bubbling wounds flung

across torsos down thighs like frozen cloth over backs
    faces
a patch of boiling skin so abstract .
its patterns are your mother's face
or animals or an arm of twilit Cape Cod beach
embracing smooth water

Photograph: silent cloud mushrooming on your fat stem
caught swallowing whatever lived beneath you
the newsreel slows
how amazing harmless and beautiful you are in silence
as you blossom and rise and take everything with you
in the murky theatre on the screen.

———

To feel another's pain—
as a passenger in an airplane for the first time hesitates
to look out the porthole
then looks, because being afraid is childish, and sees the
    earth as
a wrinkled map interrupted by clouds, merely beautiful—
is, I suppose, human. Girlish, harmless, and beautiful.

If we stay up this far long enough we will stop on the
    moon.
The prisoners' faces glow like the moon
on any night in almost any weather—
in the photographs, though a few plead
or grimace or leer or seem to be finishing an urgent
    sentence—
heads jutting, eyes wide, half-smiling, half-open
    mouths—
the rest look drained of feeling, their faces ashen,
their souls fully resigned,
convinced,

surrendered to the endlessness of death,
abandoned by all of us.
They lean out at us,
their gray, ascetic faces
a shade darker than new snow,
than that star I saw watching us.

And what we know is
those God tore away from us
get along very well without us
until, until

———

In my book, *Plantain,*
I said I kept silent for weeks,
I sat on a stone by the sea,
"my last tie with the sea is broken,"
I saw the reddish moon
enter the branches of a single pine, pass through,
be there again between twigs, needles, until

you stood near me,
glimmer of identity, soul,
whatever makes men free,

we touched, we became one voice

like a lover on whose face
the sad accident of moonlight continues.

3/

O it's so haggard, the face of the moon! Blurry
with clouds, it gilds each bleak slope of the hill
in papery light. Six places at my table
and one, only one empty—

my husband and I and our friends
celebrating, seeing the New Year in.
Why are my fingers stained with blood?
The wine scorches my throat. Why?

The host picks up his glass; it's full.
The host is very serious, doesn't move.
"Drink to the soil of our own forests,
drink to the clearings, where we lie."

Trees. Whenever I catch a glimpse of them
at the window, I stop listening, look away, I see
them and the moon as one, one old, pale,
truthful, speechless couple, at peace.

My face. One of my friends
studies it and sees, remembers— God knows what—
and shouts "Drink to her lines,
drink to the poems, where we live."

And one steps out into the night, unable
to understand, and waits in the piney darkness
and looks up and, reading my mind, calls back to us
"Drink to the one who still is not with us."

I was raised in silence and routine
in a cool nursery at the beginning of a sick age.
Something was in that room with me,
shaking my crib, and continents away— it changed the
    world.
There were voices, men's voices, arguing,
and the cottony, hollow shock of shells.
And laughter, sobbing: each sounded like the other.
Everything about it now is fantasy
except this: I loved the willow most, a tree
that lived with me all its life.
Its branches dripped green ribbon;
I used to stare into those long, thin leaves,
unfocus, let the emptiness of things
be. Strange— it died before I did.
A stump's there now, yellowish-green sprouts
inhabiting its hacked, brown top,
and I hear voices, pretending to agree.
I also hear, I think, willows
where I sit watching the unknowable sky
in a trance, taking in live stars, dead stars— you see
    both—
until my mind is nothing but the sky.
Silence. The old chill of that whitewashed room
    returns—
light coming, coming, coming—
all the years here, now, because truth cracks rock,
earth, trees, whole countries, anything heavy.

Thread

I rake the hotbed straw,
I look left half a mile downhill
where the dull green pond

shimmers. Dirt circles it, a raw, wide swath.
Even from this far I can see
creamy scum squirming inside

along the edge. The pond's a squarish oval.
Lamps, chairs, books: what's man-made barely has
    a smell.
I think I hear a little boy singing,

I think of the blackness of night, of one
especially when you never came back.
My face still feels like your face, when I think of you.

A chill floats in.
I've piled daisies in every corner of the house,
heaped vegetables in bowls, on tables;

you gone, this silence— it will never end—
my lines desolate— they can't reach you;
now the deep blue shape of each lapel is

here again as I stitch them onto the notched collar,
now the brass, eagle-figured buttons, stripes, insignia,
the weeks it took to finish, weeks when snow

stopped, fell, stopped then fell, fell endlessly:
red splashes, frozen mules, my needle whisking thread
through wool, air, sky . . . even God!

How can I write unless your dying guides my hand.
Touch me. Snow makes the silence ominous, holy. Not
    a flake is mine.
No story, no elegy. Nothing to explain.

All I need is to say to you—
without hope, without fear, in one cold line—
28 bullet holes in the last uniform I sewed.

Back

Why aren't you happy, why can't you see
our first night, infinite as the sky, is back?
We're in it now, tonight. Look—
every detail is just as it was then:

steam curls out from under the squeaky sliding doors
        of the stable,
our slow river, Moika, glides between misty banks,
the moon, as if it chose to, fades to a patch of gauze,
and I can't tell where we'll go.

Unless it's to that yawning, wooden hotel,
reeking of mildew and shellac, by the lake. It was empty.
Three lamps on, only three— to hide the lost elegance
of threadbare linen, battered oak. One waiter stood by.

Marsavo Park? Hills of ice guard it,
Kanavka Canal slides under a crystal skin . . .
if my heart stutters with fear and joy,
if your voice explodes next to me

like some unnamed, miraculous bird
that has come out of nowhere to touch me, if the
        blinding, powdery snow
seems companionable, glazed by a light no one can
        explain,
and turns silver and consoles, who's luckier than I?

Tashkent Blossoms, 1944

This city is all light, as if a king
waved his hand and was obeyed. Every window throbs
    with it, every street.
I look up into it, I live.
Is it real? How can we eat when there's war, how can
    we live?

The anxious breath of mothers is easier to understand
than what they say. These days I see
so many of them kissing their children, see
our pocked, useless fields and gutted houses.

If you sit still, don't move, don't say anything,
you'll hear the last of the railroad guns lobbing
shells seventy-five miles into those fields,
see children playing in craters three storeys deep.

But I will see
crisp, twisted, brown-crusted rolls of bread shining
in the hands of young mothers even after I die.
They fed their children. They had long, clean hair.

Bezhetsk

Stark, echoing, peeling churches, nobody at prayer,
ice drips wherever I look,
yellow and blue cornflowers splash the hills—
my son's eyes, eyes of the boy I love!

These luminous Russian nights, yearning with stars,
trouble the ancient town— no faith, nothing, no
more than the sickle moon, fixed up there.
Where did he go?

Plains fume beyond the river. Dry snow
gusts in off them, hissing against windows and walls;
men drink and dance and sing— despair, pity!—
angels celebrating the day God was born.

I know: they have dusted and washed and tidied
everything in the best room: his room; all the wicks
beneath the icons have been lit; the Bible,
closed, fat, good, lurks on the dining-room table,

and as I stand here memories begin
like a few coins that shine in an opening hand,
looking precise, as always, stern, ordering me
to go up, their famous, blank gazes judging me.

I climb the stairs.
I touch the terrifying door, once, but I will not go in.
The whole town fills with the ecstatic, tinny
hymn of the Christmas bells.

Lynx-eyed Asia, you looked into my soul
and saw something— secret, sacred, furious,
it tortures me
like the heat at noon in Termezsk.
You teased it out.
Silence hums in its veins— it *is* silence—
that noiselessness in bed in the dark
just after a mosquito passes, comes back
and buzzes in your ear—
here before us, it will always be here:
Being: all that's left
in the eyes of the homeless, jailed, defenseless ones
without family:
what God is to us in this century.
God, when we pray to you, pray to us,
prove we need each other, live the way we do,
come down and share— when we have nothing more
        to say—
what it is to be human, what it is
to live in this dying country.
Each taste of love I've ever had oozes
into my conscience like lava
simmering beneath my door.
Crackling, spitting it breaks in.
I drink every one of my own tears from invisible hands.

You can't frighten me by saying Fate's dangerous,
by talking about the boredom of the great North.
I'm miles from the city now, almost asleep on the grass
    beside you
for the first time,
and I hear everybody I know call this weekend of ours
    Goodbye.
I feel your thighs pressing all along the front of
    my thighs,
my face swims in the hollows of your neck,
my hands are in your hair.
There's the smell of you and the earth— mortal,
    overwhelming!
So we won't see dawn swelling the fields again all that
    easily;
so the moon won't take its old path over us here.
Today I'm still going to give you
things no one else was ever able to—
my face and breasts alive in the water
late at night when the stream won't let me sleep,
that sour, childish frown of helplessness
when a star vanishes and can't be brought back.
But best of all this tired, cracked voice, this echo
that was once liquid and young,
that soothed you and made you hear—
till you stopped shivering—
crows chattering all over Moscow, and made October
fresher than May. Then,
the raised, three-pointed brass stars on the plugs in the
    cannon muzzles
still gleamed. Oh remember me, my angel

of the hope and hopelessness that make love possible,
remember me.
I hate the paralyzing snow.

This Cold

The skis won't creak again
on the dry snow—
a scowling moon pinned to a blue sky,
the gently steepening meadow— I know, I know.

Windows are faces in the distance.
I can't find a track or a path,
only the black ice holes go anywhere.
It's good here.

The snow is like a simple wedding gown.
Ski tracks cross it— stitches—
and the image of us risking ourselves one night
hand in hand years back returns.

Now nothing but this cold, these walls, this snow,
this ordinary place, this patient mind.
I see whatever is here, in front of me, inside me;
I don't look beyond.

Anyone who sees my eyes
knows that immediately and feels
heavier than a parent staring into its dead
child's eyes, and sees

memory: a stone at the bottom of my soul.
Men change to things, conscious, brutal things
that kill. My sorrow's everywhere
because you're a memory, because you're lost.

The roof of stars will never go out.
I wish I were ill. I am very calm.

This life is so glorious I could even forget
the night we went crazy and lay down next to each other
in the snow.

Each minute what I hear is you—
summer, winter—
when I sit down to write.
Now the sky is blue, blue, transparent glass,
sea-blue where the sea, down to the placid floor, is clear.
Someone practices the guitar,
someone writes. But who?
This perfect, blank page *was*
perfect and blank minutes ago.
I look out the window at the sea;
it changes; it stays the same;
no one paces the dunes.
Reeds. Gray hollows. Whitecaps. My ragged braids.
Snow hoods the grasses; the trees look dead; I hear
men yelling at their sheep, a child's cry,
cedars thrashing outside my door.
Love's nothing, love is
what a schoolgirl hopes will prove she's beautiful
when she's alone.

These days before spring I'm amazed at how light my
        body is,
I don't even recognize my own house:
that instrument, that breeze, those men, water—
coming from nowhere, going nowhere—
enter me like my breath.
I watch the black-limbed alder.
Sun splashes through it like wine from a pitcher.
And God?

I see myself, and you—
one face in the mirror, seeking us, younger, at sunrise

or at night, kissing, the wet of our mouths one mouth,
our whole bodies touching— and hear:
"You wouldn't sleep with me. You wouldn't let me kiss
    your breasts.
You were stupid; afraid; beautiful; you knew nothing.
Day and night are the same. I can't find a letter,
not one word we spoke remains. Couldn't you see
the ghosts we were, even then? Didn't you know
we'd disappear?"

Fragment, 1959

And entering towns the guns had missed,
towns out of storybooks,
we saw the constellation of the Snake
but we were afraid to look at each other.

The earth smelled like an orphanage— potatoes,
disinfectant, shoes— I believed faceless
Time walked beside us: years, centuries.
And someone shook a tambourine, someone we couldn't
    see.

There were noises and tiny bluish-yellow lights.
What did they mean, those fireflies
signaling to us, beckoning? We stopped.
I even thought those noises were the lights.

Then we walked on together. I was with you, you were
    with me.
It was like that dream I had: the corpse of an old man
shone in the dark, a baby clung to his chest, both
    wrapped in a cocoon.
I could see the twitchy, delicate, wax-like hands of
    the baby

dabbling at the man's chin. The moon slid out,
suddenly. We met, we said goodbye.
If you remember that night, as I do,
wherever you are now, whatever fate

steers your life, know what I know: the time
we had was sacred like a great king's dream

turned by his people into a myth they use
to keep from believing life is a dream.

Whatever I looked at was alive, everything had a voice,
but I never found out: were you a friend, an enemy,
was it winter, summer? Smoke, singing, midnight heat.
I wrote thousands of lines. Not one told me.

After Sophocles' Death

When the eagle plummeted out of heaven
and perched on Sophocles' roof,
when the cicada's boring whine
filled his garden,
he was already a soul
crouched just outside the enemy camp,
the walls of his native city
rising behind him. Genius, immortality,
those words were as alive
as birds or insects or a mortal man.
That was when the king had a strange dream:

Dionysus told him to attack, silently,
so nothing would spoil the burial,
so the Athenians' joy
in honoring Sophocles would be as great
as what Oedipus felt when he saw his wife
swaying from a silken cord tied to a rafter—

the noon sun staring from her two gold brooches—

a mood something like what scorched the air
between the walls and the sleeping camp,
a mood like the nothingness we are.

In the Evening

1

I almost never think about you, I don't care
what happens to you now, but the wound of our meetings
hasn't healed. I still walk past your red house in the sun
above the muddy river where you live peacefully.

On blue evenings I try to predict the future
like a witch. I have a feeling we'll meet again.
Two monks pass slowly along the top of an old
    castle wall.
All day the bells have tolled over the endless,
    plowed fields.

2

There's a line between people, a secret margin that being
    in love
or passion can't cross even when lips bite each other
and the heart is smashed by love, in pure silence. It's
    unbearable!

Friendship can't do anything there,
neither can the years of fiery, narrow happiness
when the soul's free and doesn't feel the slow boredom
    of flesh.

Anyone who tries to cross that line is insane,
those who reach it are punished by despair.
Now you know why your hands don't cover my breasts.

3

I almost never dream about you now,
I don't see you the way I used to, everywhere,

mist has blocked off the white road,
shadows keep jumping across the water.

I'm cutting off all the branches of the lilac bushes
that don't have flowers. I want
the tame, knowable, physical world that can't see me.
God has cured me with the icy calm of not loving.

In Two

I'm empty. Not seeing you, staying away
is too mysterious, a victory
composed of unspoken phrases, unknown words,
glances that can't stop questioning these walls,
glances that can't stop looking at your glance.
I go outside. It's beautiful near evening. Red hills.
Only inches between the first few stars.
I go back in. I almost see you, I reach out.
Only tears say what existence means.
A wild rose bush near Moscow
is still part of this, is these colorless words,
God knows why.

I sit.here, envisioning people on the beach.
They shift their bodies every few minutes, they turn
like seals in the sun. Do those hulks live
for reasons other than why *we* persist,
as they believe, hope, cling to each other, search
one darkness or the other: physical, metaphysical?
I know— those last two words aren't opposite
these days, but that's something I can't explain.
Let those vacationers in Paradise
loll on the broiling sand. It's cold here.
I scour these walls to tell you what is mine:

memory without image: that sacred, last time we did not
     meet:
inside me: still, unassailable, useless flame of my triumph
     over fate.

Alone

No one can hurt me. They've tried to kill me
so many times that nobody frightens me now.
I know what kind of people want me dead:
fanatics in love, political, dressed up to look poor.
Nothing they can do is hidden from me.
This ordinary room of mine
is Paradise, cut off, a stone box
that overlooks my old street, people I used to know.
There's so little in it— two chairs,
bed, table, books, a red Persian prayer rug
with a cross in a golden field in the middle.
It could be called a trap; maybe it is.
But what I feel
is gratitude— to those who put me here
and, in their way, hung doors, cemented brick, glazed
    windows;
may they never be ill or worried; may life pass them by.
I'm up this morning with the workers, I see
my face in the streaked mirror, bleached with anxiety,
and what I am is what the sun is—
itself free of itself daily
even when its last shard of light eases under the rim of
    the earth.
Everything's dark. Whenever I shut my eyes.
I look outside; turn back;
look in the mirror and see
the small window, reflected:
pines miles away across a field,
a road, one cloud, clumps of bluish mist, some dead
    machine
slouched in a gown of rust— nature, things dropping
    back to nature,

me noticing my face among it all.
I tie one short ribbon in my gray hair
and step back— so much younger than the face I see—
nowhere, homeless, peaceful,
and speak to the voice inside me that answers me.
Sometimes I only sit here. Winds from a frozen sea
come through the open window. I don't get up, I
don't close it. I let the air touch me. I begin to freeze.
Twilight or dawn, the same pink streaks of cloud.

A dove pecks wheat from my extended hand,
those infinite, blind pages, stacked on my table . . .

some desolate urge lifts my right hand, guides me.
Much much older than I am, it comes down,
easy as an eyelid, godless, and I write.

My Door

A face or leg
on the frieze under the green roof of the customs
    building
caught my eye
and I saw the striped, weather-beaten flag;
its frayed, leading edge was a rainbowy blue-black blur,
a halyard clanked on the pole.
The orange haze that drifts up off the river
in late spring, usually, still dimmed the streets.
The sky was a watery green, the flag kept heaving and
    snapping;
I was afraid, suspicious, and held my breath.
I remember, too,
seeing myself as a child at the seashore,
my bare feet cool, sliding around in cracked leather
    shoes,
my braided hair
coiled back in a tight, shiny, coal-hard knot.
No images of death.
I was running; whatever filled my head
I sang; I saw myself
looking out my door
at the plump, silvery, turnip-shaped domes of the
    Chersonese temple,
glowing above all the houses,
and I thought
not to have fame and happiness is a worse despair
than loving them, these vices, as much as I do.

I think of the gentleness of snow, I see us
stop and hold each other. Raw, night air.
The sting of blown snow. Hollowness. Guns.

A dream of being somewhere else,
in a leveled city, that feels when I wake
as if I will never be the same now
but can't explain why, can't get up,
and when I do, finally, in the sluggish, bleary dawn,
can't recognize at first, looking into
the mirror above the sink, who it is: that flag—
I still sense its agony—
and the face and leg
(what's left of a story
about heroes, wives, chariots, battle scenes)
connected to no one
up there in the blurred stone,
down here among us,

some happiness annihilating us, stealing our identity
as I stand here— belonging to the face that looks into
    my face—
saying this.

Endings

I can barely speak
but I still have things to say;
not being in love is a relief.
There's nothing between me and the sky;
it starts at the hills, it shelters everything, it
goes on and on.
I think. I plan. With purity.
Books, paperweights, bunches of old drafts
flow with the world, flow with what's in my mind.
Not to withhold oneself is clarity.
Not to need safety
as the nothingness grows. . . .

These nights I sleep.
Insomnia nurses someone else.
When I look back to find *him,* to see *it,*
nothing's there. The black
iron hands on the tower clock
aren't arrows now.
That's how it is: everything is what it is— light.
I'm free, I forgive, forgive all, I live
without beliefs, looking at the sun— past dawn now—
flash on patches of wet ivy until it blinds me.

Dandelions like words follow a low wood fence.
Some cluster against a post, some stray between.
One story ends, another begins,
mine, yours, everyone's.
And fear: each brick on each pale house looks paler,
nothing is warm;
an ambulance's crazed, multiple wail
drifts in on fog and incense,

me re-creating this, believing this, being this
as if she and I were the same,
speaking in my third-floor room.

Don't you see us on the shelled road that May night?
Each inch in front of us was a wall.
The ditches whispered. Carnations. I thought
all Asia smelled like that—
blood, steel carcasses, fire—
but I was hallucinating, happiness
broke like a flare above the trenches,
war forced it into my soul,
war and the craziness of love.

Now autumn eats its way in. Wild frilly
puffs of mildew staining a wall, ecstasy, tenderness,
glances, a handshake or brown leaf—

anything could end this:
who is it, I or you?

I lift my face— close; closer.
The phrases blur, the blur
rises from silence into silence,
each syllable echoing,
each touch a resurrected meaning.
I roll this page backwards in the machine
to make it disappear, then spin it back
and see the emptiness around, between
each letter, word, and line.
I feel the eyes of whatever is here
watch me. I watch what watches me.

Books packed on sagging shelves, the unending red brick
    houses

of my childhood, of my life now, row on row,
where a bum sits whittling
on a neighbor's steps, yards piled with bedsprings,
legless chairs, branches the poor are saving.

I move my lips.
The sky is a hard blue.
Death's death. There's no sleep at the end,
no waking as I woke to these words—
don't you see us?—
no bringing-back to life. Only this voice,
continuing here above Mt. Vernon Street,
only these accidental words.
I listen.

Don't you see us— a soul, a brightness?

On the wall day
splashes a pane of light. Through it
we are taken.

Afterword

Not translations or versions or imitations, these poems started several years ago when I read Richard McKane's translations of Anna Akhmatova's poetry in his *Selected Poems of Anna Akhmatova*. The first ones I wrote *were* versions and appeared in *Grief: Poems and Versions of Poems*, but soon after that something drew me back to his book (and to a few scattered in anthologies) and I found myself working with his English on other, freer poems, and on rewriting the ones from *Grief*.

Some affinity must have driven me, so I clung to that impulse, stayed with it, and wrote until, most of the time, I could barely remember those English originals or trace the debt I owed. Often I simply let revision dictate changes from draft to draft. Now and then I would go back—rarely in the late drafts—to get help from his book. Finally I wrote the poems as my own, as a single, binding work. (I have come to see *The Black Gates* as a long poem in sections or poems which can be read and understood separately, its longest part—its hub—the poem *Memory*, which has as one of its themes the structure of the book itself.) But I know they are based on a voice I sense is doubly mine: love and loss in myself and in another—the mixture is infinite, the many sources unclear.

I treated this streak of writing as infinite until it ended. Halfway through I lost all sense of whose poetry it was—hers, mine—or at least I felt that such a definition would not matter to the poetry. I even wrote without starting from the English texts. *Memory*, the longest poem in the book, isn't the title of one of Akhmatova's poems, and that poem is mostly mine from beginning to end, by invention, by reference to passages I remembered and changed, and by the theft along the way of a few short passages from an unpublished manuscript of poetry by Akhmatova, translated by Mr. McKane.

We would like to escape from autobiography, especially these days after so much "confessional" poetry has appeared, been misdefined, and is being condemned. *Four Quartets* is no less confessional than *Life Studies* or *Song of Myself*. Jung's "curse of personality" is at the heart of both; both have that individuality of feeling and depth of sincerity that Tolstoi rightly demanded of authentic art. To forget oneself, to avoid one's special pettiness—fine. But in content, rhythm, "heart's tone," we are always there, whether we call ourselves "I," "you," or the name of a fictional character, or invent part of ourselves by speaking through a mask; whether we narrate without ever mentioning ourselves, creating our own absence in other people, events, things. I think I believed, dimly at the time, that I was being released from myself by these poems when, in fact, I was merely discovering, hearing from a part of myself I did not remember or yet know. Or was I forging a new degree of awareness beyond the identity I knew? Or was I, as Herb Mason suggests in a letter, helped by a ghost?

Beginning with other texts is sometimes a way of managing the forbidden. It provides that mask (or is it a mirror?) through which we may speak directly without being seen. It is like a mirror without glass in it, an approach to knowledge which leads us finally—like a ritual of purification—into that state of hopelessness which introduces us to the most saddening of all our misperceptions—necessary as it may be—of time: personal identity. In these poems, and elsewhere, I hope for an identity of truths, not an identity of self-images.

I feel close to what I sense is Akhmatova's love of the everyday, to how she and nature seem to express themselves through each other, to her sensitivity to loss, to the unity of personal and political fact which grew more and more necessary to the way she saw life. I admire her ability to be alone, and, at the same time, to be honest about its graces and pains. I imagine I was working at myself when I wrote these poems, and so I suspect there must be, however slight, some temperamental connection between us, if only as I invented it for the poems. But, as I have suggested, I do not really know her work. I kept hearing this voice, and I wrote it down.

Stephen Berg

66 /

Acknowledgments

I'm grateful to Howard Moss, whose constant, enthusiastic encouragement was essential to the poems, and to my friends Jeff Marks and Charlie Williams. Charlie and Jeff made suggestions which deeply influenced late drafts of the poems, as they have done many times with other work of mine.

For the generous assistance of a joint grant from AID, Inc. and the Dietrich Foundation I wish to thank Jerome J. Shestack and Mr. and Mrs. Daniel W. Dietrich, III. The truth is I could never have found the energy to develop the book, from its first inklings in *Grief* to its form here, without the help of Jennie and Dan Dietrich and Jerry Shestack, whose grant allowed me to take a sabbatical from my teaching duties.

To Tom Stewart and Ellen Posner for their support while I finished the first stages of some of these, my thanks.

I also want to thank the John Simon Guggenheim Memorial Foundation and the National Endowment for the Arts for awarding me fellowships on which I wrote some of the early stages of these poems.

Larry Lieberman, my editor, has treated the book and me with such care, intelligence, and trust that I do not know how to thank him fully. And Hayden Carruth's generosity and critical advice have arrived to help always at those difficult, right times when they were most needed.

Most of these poems take off from Richard McKane's translations in his *Selected Poems of Anna Akhmatova* (Penguin Books, 1969). My Afterword sketches this process. My book title is the same as the title of a poem in *Grief: Poems and Versions of Poems* (Viking, 1975). That poem is about my early experience reading Akhmatova's work in English.

Poetry from Illinois

History is Your Own
Heartbeat
Michael S. Harper (1971)

The Foreclosure
Richard Emil Braun (1972)

The Scrawny Sonnets
and Other Narratives
Robert Bagg (1973)

The Creation Frame
Phyllis Thompson (1973)

To All Appearances: Poems
New and Selected
Josephine Miles (1974)

Nightmare Begins
Responsibility
Michael S. Harper (1975)

The Black Hawk Sings
Michael Borich (1975)

The Wichita Poems
Michael Van Walleghen (1975)

Cumberland Station
Dave Smith (1977)

Tracking
Virginia R. Terris (1977)

Poems of the Two Worlds
Frederick Morgan (1977)

Images of Kin: New and
Selected Poems
Michael S. Harper (1977)

On Earth As It Is
Dan Masterson (1978)

Riversongs
Michael Anania (1978)

Goshawk, Antelope
Dave Smith (1979)

Death Mother and Other
Poems
Frederick Morgan (1979)

Local Men
James Whitehead (1979)

Coming to Terms
Josephine Miles (1979)

Searching the Drowned Man
Sydney Lea (1980)

With Akhmatova at the
Black Gates
Stephen Berg (1981)